STEPPING INTO VERSE

BY

HUGH TIMOTHY

FIRE CIRCLE
PUBLISHING

First published in Great Britain 1995
By MGSC
Second edition 1996
Reset to new format with amendments
Reprinted with amendments 1997

New expanded edition 2014
Published by Fire Circle Publishing

ISBN: 978-0-9930313-0-4

Copyright © Hugh Timothy
The right of Hugh Timothy to be identified as the author of this work has been asserted by him in accordance with the Copyright, Design and Patents Act, 1988
Cover design and photograph © Timothy Jenkins with help from Jones' Creative Services Ltd.

All rights reserved. No part of this publication may be reproduced, distributed, or transmitted in any form or by any means, including photocopying, recording, or other electronic or mechanical methods, without the prior written permission of the publisher, except in the case of brief quotations embodied in critical reviews and certain other noncommercial uses permitted by copyright law. For permission requests, write to :-
Fire Circle Publishing,
9a Craddocks Parade,
ASHTEAD,
Surrey
KT21 1QL

Printed in the UK by Jones' Creative Services Ltd

Dedication

I would like to delicate this book to Friends and family y Poets, Stella Stocker of the WEA and all the friends I have made within those groups and the support and encouragement that they have given me but especially John Lemmon without whose guidance and scholarship I would not be writing to-day, and Morag Hale for some concederable help preparing this book for press.

ACKNOWLEDGMENTS

The Ffrig Of Frogimar *was joint winner in the StoryPods International Competition for Nonsense Verse 2010*

The Push *Previously published in Retort issue 1 1996*

CONTENTS

Moments……………………………………………..………...9
A Favourite Spot…………………………………………….11
The Visitation……………………………………………….13
The Parting……………………………………………….…20
The Parting…………………………………………………..21
Composition…………………………………………………..21
A Meeting with the Muses……………………………….22
The Wild "Heart"………………………………….…..…..25
The Ffrig Of Frogimar……………………………….....…27
Sanctuary…………………………………………….……..29
To Music…………………………………………………….30
I wish I'd said that at the time………………………….31
A Moment in war…………………………………....……33
The Push…………………………………………………….35
The Fence……………………………………………....……37
Pentire from Tristram…………………………………….39
Midsummer Madness………………………………….….41
Vision……………………………………………………..….43
The Tale of Eskimo Pete……………………………….….45
Polzeath Possessive……………………………….....…….47
La Pucelle……………………………………………....…..49
A Legend of St Cecilia……………………………....…….51
Bye-Bye Blackbird………………………………………….59

5

WAY IN

Readers often ignore prefaces as they can tend to be a bit long and boring. In the hope of tempting you to read this I shall keep it brief.

There were four main objectives in my mind when compiling this collection of my work. These were:

1. That it should be a family book.
2. That it should be rich in variety.
3. That it should attract new converts to verse.
4. That it should be honest.

Contained within *Stepping into Verse* is some of my earliest verse, some items dating back 40 years or more. This is one reason why I chose the title. Those early poems represent my first steps into verse. My wish that the book might introduce others to the fun and joy of verse was my second reason for the title.

Often, when I read poetry, I feel I would like to know the story behind the verse; how it came to be written. I believe that knowing this can increase one's understanding of the verse. So to make this collection a bit different I decided to do just that.

The poems are not set in any chronological order, and whilst their arrangement is not altogether random, the connection between one item and another is occasionally somewhat tenuous and abstract.

Thanks.

If you have read this far then it was probably long enough.

HUGH TIMOTHY

September 1995

Sometimes life can become a habit rather than an experience. One day quite recently I suddenly became aware of the rut that I had become stuck in. I realized that my life had become a habit. Some where along the line I had forgotten how to live. The "poetry" and vitality had gone out of my life and I had sunk into a slough of tedium.

I felt like a child awakening to Christmas morning, full of anticipation for the day ahead. I stopped work, (being self employed I could) and took a walk in the country near where I live. As I gazed across the rolling Surrey countryside around the Dorking gap, the joy at finding what I had lost burst open within me. I wrote Moments there and then.

MOMENTS

How happy I, with grateful eye,
To see the world so green.
To glory in the amber's shine
In blues celestial, divine,
Absorbing nature's rich design
With joy serene.

And then to feel the careless wind
That shakes and stirs the scene.
To feel it rising from the still:
The fluttering leaves and turning mill.
Through rippling grasses on the hill
Its dance is seen.

And all about in harmony
With nature's rustling sound,
The distant bleating lambs of spring,
The skylark's joy upon the wing,
The descant to which all birds sing
Brings peace profound.

Through childhood and youth I had often walked the lanes over what is known locally as Norbury Park and Fetcham Common. They had always been a source of adventure, delight and imagination for me. In childhood the "Wild West" was transplanted here and Robin Hood's merry men waited in ambush in the timeless oaks and beeches. Here, and in a few other special places, in particular parts of Cornwall, of which I'll say more later, there exists for me a timeless and magical quality.

It was thinking of favourite places that brought the next poem into mind. The idea of a place you go to find your soul and recharge your batteries is probably one we all share.

A Favourite Spot

He leant upon the gate and gazed
And thought of life.
Life wasn't fair,
And no one understood.
Dad least of all
And Mum just smiled.
They didn't know - how could they?

The years rolled on.

He leant upon the gate and gazed
And thought of life,
And life was full
Of joy and love and pain.
He loved her so!
Did she love him?
What did it hold - their future?

The years rolled on.

He leant upon the gate and gazed
And thought of life.
And Death had knocked
His father, then his Ma.
The rolling years
Were racing now.
Nowhere to run - and no escape.

The years rolled on

He leant upon the gate and gazed
And thought of life,
His Dad and Ma
Seemed somehow closer now.
The past was full
To overflow.
His life seemed ripe and ready to be picked.

They found him by the gate.

Ideas for verse come in all sorts of ways. Sometimes an idea for a subject is born of an event. Other times a line just comes into your head and the poem grows from that. The Visitation started with the first line which seemed to ask for a story. It is a fantasy set vaguely in the middle ages.

THE VISITATION

or

THE LEGEND OF THE BARON'S ARMOUR

"Bollocks!" bawled the Baron as he bounced out of bed.
"Beg your pardon", said the Bishop who had turned a trifle red.
"Do you wish me to repeat myself", the Baron blandly said.
"I said, BOLLOCKS, My Lord Bishop" and he bipped him on the head.

I think it only fair to say in bold Lord John's defence,
But for one or two exceptions he was normally a placid man.
Both honest to himself and God he boldly scorned pretence.
In particular deception made him very much the acid man.

If you met him as a stranger,
I feel sure you would agree,
That you could not meet a nicer
Nor more friendly man than he.

It was of course the kind and gen'rous nature of the peer
That so markedly contrasted with his temper when he let it loose,
And filled the unsuspecting fool with deep and abject fear,
So fiercely to be blasted by his temper and his foul abuse.

These outbursts were so very rare,
Or so I understand,
They could easily be counted
On the fingers of one hand.

There are little pet aversions that we all find hard to take,
And amicable Baron's are the same.
I'm sure that you could name a few that tend to make you shake
With a fury that's impossible to tame.

Lord John had eaten well that night,
And drunk with gay abandon.
Consuming all with rare delight
That he could lay his hand on.

And so about the midnight hour
The board was clear - the fire was dead.
The guests had left the Baron's tower
And John, himself, had left for bed.

His gourmand feast had made its mark,
For now his earnest wish was sleep
The candles snuffed, the chamber dark,
He soon fell into slumber deep.

It must have been at least three hours or so
The Baron slept with foghorn snores.
When suddenly he woke to sounds below
Of shouts and yells and banging doors.

Bolt upright in his bed the Baron sat,
Gathering his robes about him tight,
Sifting each sound to learn from this or that
What rude affront had so disturbed his night.

He did not have too long to wait.
His chamber door burst open wide.
His servant Dickon, at a rate,
Crashed in - The Bishop at his side.

The Baron stared in wonder at the pair;
A panting Bishop with his robes awry;
A servant mouthing soundless to the air,
And both of them with wild and staring eye.

"Well" said the Baron as he looked at each in turn
"'Tis a strange time to be calling, you'll agree.
Perhaps you'll have the kindness to explain what grave concern
Merits waking me at quarter after three."

The Bishop, with a super human struggle was the first
To compose himself to any marked degree.
Rejecting all propriety he let his story burst
On the company with nothing short of glee.

"We've had a visitation from the heavens, good m'lord.
Oh it's difficult to know where to begin -
To describe the awesome spectacle we've witnessed and afford
An explanation for so rudely bursting in.

As we journeyed home this evening from the banquet we espied,
Not seven miles beyond your very door,
Some little lights that travelled at some speed and side by side
Across the midnight sky 'bove yonder moor.

At first sighting we dismissed them as some comets and we might
Have thought no more about them and gone home,
Till to our great surprise and consternation at the sight,
They changed their path across the heavenly dome.

Fear gripped our very souls, the sight transfixing every one.
The lights came down towards our little band.
We could not even find the strength one needs to turn and run,
As the bright lit objects settled down to land.

My entourage then broke and fled but for a faithful few.
The rest of us stayed crouching in the trees,
Till natural curiosity eventually won through
And we started creeping forward by degrees.

I cannot tell you truly now precisely what we felt
What fear and trepidation filled each mind.
For there, not fifty yards beyond the bushes where we knelt,
Was a spectacle not easily defined.

Before us lay three mighty discs of metal burnished bright
Atop of each a dome of clearest glass.
From each of which there issued forth a powerful glaring light
That glittered bright upon the frosty grass.

Then as we gazed a magic fell upon us every one.
The world went black as dark as any night.
And when the darkness melted and the magic spell was done,
We'd been transported into heavenly light.

A wondrous world as bright as day and yet no shadow fell
And lights like fireflies flashed in rows all round
Whilst weird devises spun and whirled, too numerous to tell
And visions danced and pictures moved with sound.

And yes what sounds, what curious sounds, like music and like bird,
Like flutes and pipe and horn, like lyre and harp.
With walls that spoke with voices in a tongue I've never heard.
Sounds soft and round, sounds loud and harsh and sharp.

And there before us, all in gold, their heads in crystal bowls
Two figures, tall stood gazing at our band
What they were we could not tell, mortal or immortal souls,
Archangels, gods.... These strangers in our land.

And round their head an endless band that made their heads appear
As if their very skulls were set with gems
Revealed upon inspection a phenomenon most queer
They were but coloured eyes on little stems.

Whilst both of them appeared to have a pair of legs like us
Each arm was serpentine without a hand
Which having four on either side, just like an octopus
The sight of which left all of us unmanned.

Nor did they speak as you or I. They had no mouths to speak.
They somehow put their meaning in our minds.
But how they talked amongst themselves, it really was unique!
Through noises they produced from their behinds.

I stood up to address them in a style polite but firm
I asked them to explain just who the were
And then perhaps to say Where they had come from and affirm
Precisely their intent for being here.

They said they couldn't tell me who they were or whence they'd come.
And if they did, I wouldn't comprehend
They simply asked us questions of a private kind and some
About the way we fight and we defend.

I didn't want to tell them, so I didn't say a word
They seemed to take the answers from my head.
So I tried to think of answers that were totally absurd
But they got them from my other folk instead.

Eventually to our surprise it all went dark anew,
In just the manner it had done before.
Awake, we'd been transported to a reassuring view.
We found ourselves again upon the moor.

So we quickly fled our captors and made rapidly to you
Our running steeds much hastened by our scare,
Convinced you'd want to hear and further more know what to do
About this very troubling affair."

The Baron held the Bishop with a penetrating stare.
A breathless silence fell upon the room.
The Bishop cringed in terror 'neath that gaze that stripped him bare.
And a stillness intermingled with the gloom.

"Bollocks!" bawled the Baron as he bounced out of bed.
"Beg your pardon", said the Bishop who had turned a trifle red.
"Do you wish me to repeat myself", the Baron blandly said.
"I said, BOLLOCKS, My Lord Bishop" and he bipped him on the head.

Then the Bishop found his courage and he faced the Baron out
And stood up straight to all his five foot one.
"As a peer, a man of honour, I'm surprised that you can doubt
Your Bishop's word. Yea treat that word as fun."

"Control your fiendish temper, sir, and kindly have respect
For your Bishop, God's anointed, your confessor.
And when I've shown you proof of all I've told you, I'll expect
To see a very penitent transgressor."

For a moment it appeared as if the Baron might explode
In a raging scarlet apoplectic fit.
His eyes protruded wildly in the manner of a toad,
With both fists raised on high prepared to hit.

Perhaps it was the boldness of the Bishop or it may
Quite well have been the bishop's very gist.
For which it was I would not know or speculate to say,
Save the wondrous change in him could not be missed.

The thought at last occurred to him that he might just be wrong
In judgement of the Bishop's wondrous tale.
There was the possibility the tale though strange and long
Might still be true which made the Baron quail.

The Baron grabbed his armour and the Baron grabbed his sword
The Baron grabbed his battle-axe, the best gold could afford.
Then swinging round his battle-axe to emphasise each word,
"TO BATTLE, MY LORD BISHOP" was the battle-cry he roared.

In very little time at all the Baron's men at arms
Were roused from sleep and gathered in the yard
Whilst others were arriving from the villages and farms.
The Baron, folk all held in high regard.

'Twas a formidable army that left the castle gates.
The Baron and the bishop at their head.
The bishop's tale is quickly spread as man to man relates
Till every soldiers heart is filled with dread.

But still they marched on bravely, by their numbers fortified.
The story grew and grew each time 'twas told.
As each event was added to and grossly magnified
Pure fiction and mistakes were manifold.

They found on their arrival, to the bishop's great relief,
His story of the visitors was true.
The sight before them plainly left no room for disbelief
The discs remained quite clear for all to view.

The Baron gave instruction to surround the alien craft
At a distance within range but not too near.
And when he gave command they were to let fly fore and aft
With bolt and flaming arrow and with spear.

"I'm sure that we are stronger than the enemy" he said,
"How can so few be any match for us.
Prepare to battle boldly men. The foe will soon be bled.
Then back to bed with scarcely any fuss."

You could tell the bishop didn't share the Baron's confidence
His faith had not prepared him for such shocks.
Till certain they were men not gods, he had some evidence,
He slipped away to hide behind some rocks.

The Baron dropped his sword, a sign that battle should commence
And spears and arrows shot up through the night,
But not a single missile reached the enemy's defence
For each was blown to pieces in full flight.

A multitude of beams of light had struck the arrows down
And made the Baron's onslaught look absurd.
The Baron felt this enemy had made him look a clown
So growing fury found him undeterred.

With his battle-axe a swinging, he stepped out all alone.
An awe inspiring sight for all to see.
He marched to meet the enemy and fight them on his own.
With stoic pace he went forth valiantly.

Knowing what we think we know of those from outer space,
The outcome of this selfless act seems plain.
We already know what happened in the spears and arrows case,
So we surely can expect the same again.

The unexpected factor no one took into account,
The unsuspected wild card in the pack,
Was the history of his armour, a factor paramount
In the failure or success of John's attack.

The armour was his father's and his father's before him,
Down through the generations, it was passed.
Created by a wizard in the mists of time most dim
And in rare exotic metals it was cast.

No battle-axe had dented it no bolt had made its mark,
Impervious to everything, but rain.
So the Baron full of confidence and valour did embark
On conflict that to some might seem insane.

From every craft a stream of rays converged upon Lord John
He kept on moving forward just the same
And like the very sun itself the Baron's armour shone
Reflecting back the rays from whence they came.

The rays became more powerful and his sword was blown away.
It vaporised his battle-axe as well.
Untouched himself, the Baron still kept marching to the fray;
An angel shining at the gates of hell.

The energy reflected back was only just a part,
The armour's Magic Force retaining some,
Which changed to three great balls of power, it shot right from its heart
And blew the aliens' craft to kingdom come.

The aliens are too wary of the armour's mystic power
To ever risk attacking earth again.
Thank God the armour's secret never left the Baron's Tower.
It dissolved when some one left it in the rain.

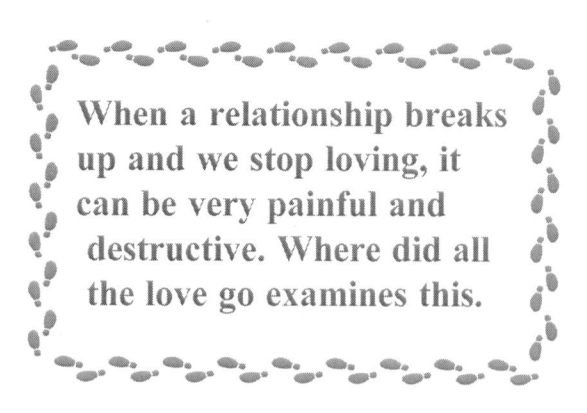

> When a relationship breaks up and we stop loving, it can be very painful and destructive. Where did all the love go examines this.

THE PARTING

Where did all the love go -
Down the drain?
It didn't go, it changed -
It changed to pain.

Where did all the pain go -
Out the gate?
It didn't go, it changed -
It changed to hate.

Where did all the hate go -
Deep distress?
It didn't go, it changed
To emptiness.

> I write music as well as verse and people ask me where the music comes from. This short verse was written in an attempt to explain.

Composition

While wandering through the spaces of my mind
I found
A sound
I took it to the keyboard and when there
I smote
A note
And from that note I made a harmony
Resound
Around
The harmony lead on and more and more
Like corn
Were born
And through this endless field a symphony
Just grew
And grew.

> A bit outrageous as I have yet to write a symphony, but it's as near as I can get to my musical source.

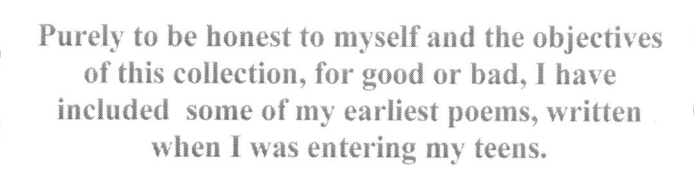

Purely to be honest to myself and the objectives of this collection, for good or bad, I have included some of my earliest poems, written when I was entering my teens.

This rather ostentatious piece was based on a teenage vision. I should laugh at the angst but I still really remember the excitement of the release of my first discovery of creative energy.

A Meeting with the Muses

a feeling within
tense and knotted
as a piece of string
of great length left loose
on the floor of my heart
in spasms pulled tight
to near breaking strain
in spasms slack
loose and useless

and then a feeling
to make me jump
spread eagle to the stars
then shatter me
to rush in multi-pieces
a hundred thousand
different crazy ways
burst the world
and strike the people dumb
by that same ecstasy
that flairs within my soul

and all to float on high
in heavenly concord
with eternal choirs
infinite in size
in endless songs
to float
and float
through great vast nothingness
and on
and on
through a thousand heavenly harbours
all being one
one being many
with cheery fishers sitting on the walls
with smiles of happiness
across their rugged faces
knowing
in their wisdom I have found
in explosive illumination
a life
which they will watch as I pass them
seated on each harbour wall
then over me as birds peculiar
and so to higher realms
until I reach to death itself
wisdom complete
life complete.

Tim Jenkins
October 1958

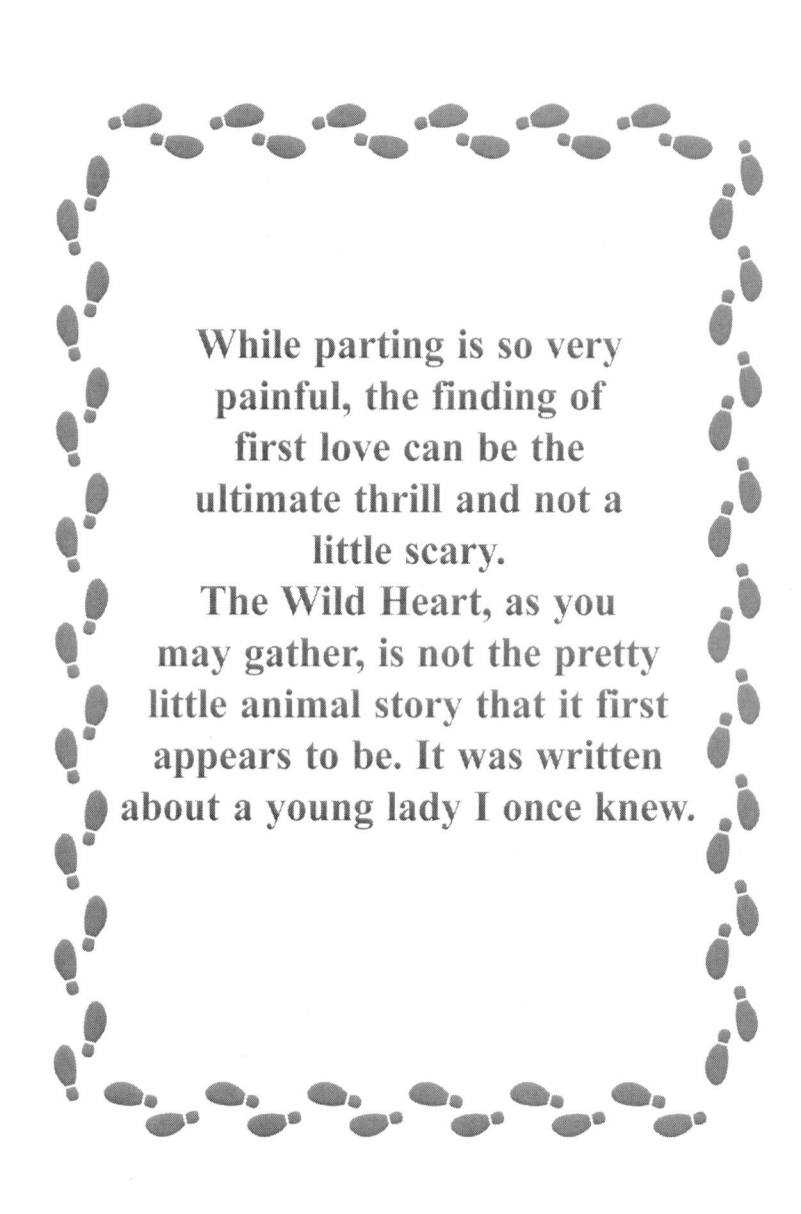

While parting is so very painful, the finding of first love can be the ultimate thrill and not a little scary.
The Wild Heart, as you may gather, is not the pretty little animal story that it first appears to be. It was written about a young lady I once knew.

THE WILD "HEART"

Wild as the roe-deer. Wild, so wild.
Wild as the wind, eternal child.
Child of the wild-world greets the day,
Seeking a funful game to play.

Nymph of the sunshine sniffs the breeze
Frolics and gallops through glades and trees
Happy a careless song she sings,
Full of the joy that living brings.

Out of the forest a male appears.
Watches the nymph in her wild careers
Gloriously free as she leaps and turns.
Then, seeing the Male, hides in the ferns.

She sees his eyes and his princely stance,
His aura of power and confidence.
A feeling grows that she can't ignore,
An emotion never felt before.

Her heart is troubled, her spirit in doubt.
She gallops and tosses her head about.
Perhaps she hopes if she dances on
She'll find that haunting feeling gone.

The male draws near and tests her scent
He falls for this wild thing heaven sent.
He fears no love could ever tame
This spirit, part of nature's flame.

Held by a strand she cannot see,
She tests it and tries it. She can't get free.
She faintly longs for her careless ways.
To run again where the river plays.

Entrapped by a love sown in her heart.
Fighting but pulls herself apart.
He hopes she'll learn that her free wild soul
Is what he loves the best of all.

At one time I was a keen thespian, but it takes nerve to go on stage and suddenly one day I lost it. I had to put my aspiration to become a great actor on the back burner. But from time to time on Wednesday nights I can be found at the Chanticleer Folk Club, The Parrot, Forest Green, near Dorking performing monologues. It is strictly a music club but I am slotted in as a sort of novelty break sometimes. I had learnt many Edwardian and late Victorian Monologues at my grandfather's knee. I performed those until I'd exhausted my repertoire and then added some modern ones and finally began slipping in some of my own poems. They were well received and I started to write some specially. The *Ffrig of Frogimar* is one of these and like *The Visitation* was born from the first line coming into my head.

THE FFRIG OF FROGIMAR

The fabled Ffrig Of Frogimar
Was sitting in a Glasgow bar,
When through the door a Purple Cat
Walked in and on a bar stool sat.
Of finest malt he bought a dram
And then performed a bold salaam
Before the Ffrig of Frogimar.
A silence fell upon the bar,
So strange the antics of the cat,
Who once more on the bar stool sat.
He ordered then another dram,
Performed again a bold salaam
Before the Ffrig of Frogimar,
Who smoked upon his green cigar
And sat in silence quite unmoved.
Reaction, which the cat reproved.
The cat drew from a gold valise
The Russian Tolstoy's War and Peace,
Which he recited in reverse,
Translated into Latin verse.
The Ffrig of Frogimar just sat,
Despite the efforts of the cat.
And all the people in the place
Just saw him talk to empty space.
For no one in a Glasgow bar
Can see the Ffrig of Frogimar.
But seeing Purple Cats Salaam
Is common where they drink the dram.

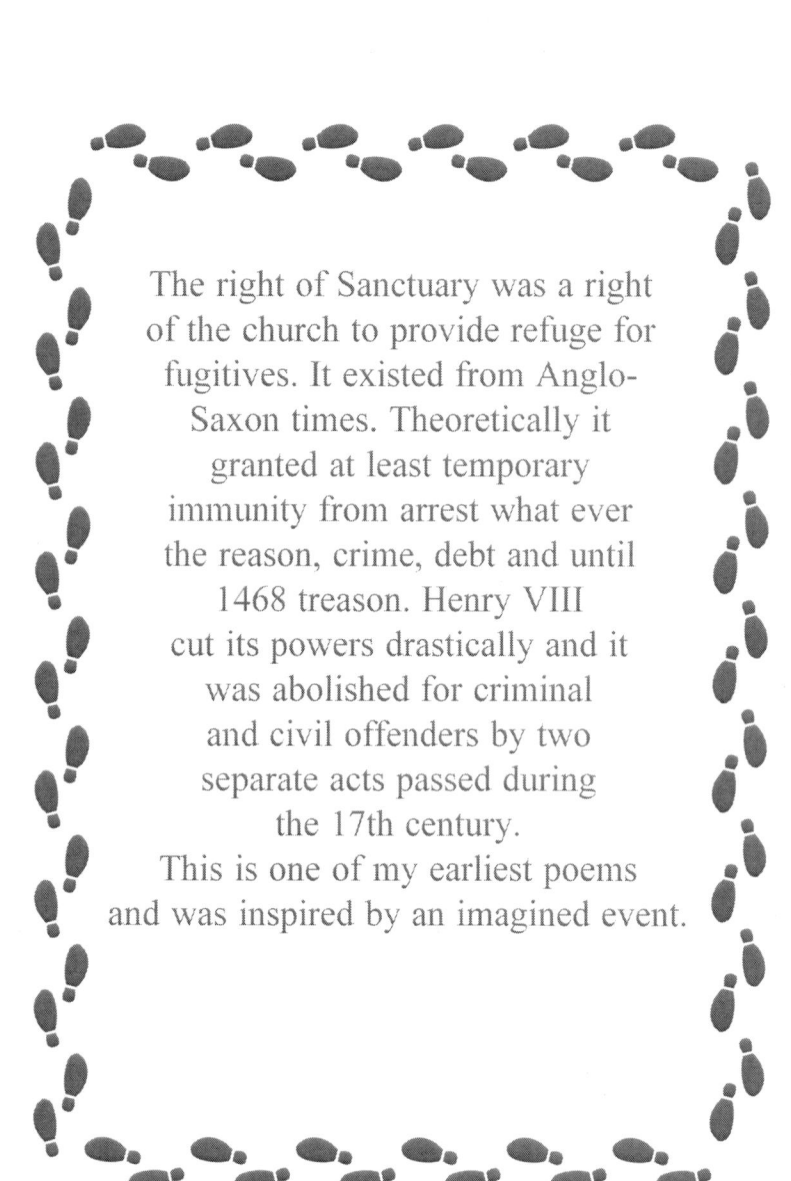

The right of Sanctuary was a right of the church to provide refuge for fugitives. It existed from Anglo-Saxon times. Theoretically it granted at least temporary immunity from arrest what ever the reason, crime, debt and until 1468 treason. Henry VIII cut its powers drastically and it was abolished for criminal and civil offenders by two separate acts passed during the 17th century.
This is one of my earliest poems and was inspired by an imagined event.

SANCTUARY

The great oak door swung open wide.
In breathless fear he crashed inside
And crumpled to the floor.
The atmosphere of peace and calm
Immersed the fear, engulfed alarm.
He stood and closed the door.

He slowly paced the tranquil aisle
On pallid face, a bitter smile.
The altar lay ahead.
The candles on the altar beamed.
Their light upon the crosses gleamed;
The gleam of hope not dead.

When at the altar's foot he bowed;
He clasped his hands and cried aloud
The tears of torture's end.
'Twas then a figure from the side,
Dressed long in black, was seen to glide.
The Cleric and the friend.

The father stood erect and straight
With empty eyes, he gazed at fate.
Again the door swung wide.
And through the door an angry crowd
Rushed in and stopped, Then cried aloud,
"'Tis here he tried to hide!"

Then silence fell. The hunters froze.
The seconds passed. The hunted rose.
And then the shout rang clear.
The Crowd with one accord came down.
The hunted grasped the priestly gown
And cringed in mortal fear.

"Father help me! Don't despise!"
But fear was in the father's eyes.
He pushed him to the floor.
They dragged him screaming from the place
With agony distorted face.
"CUT!" cried the director.

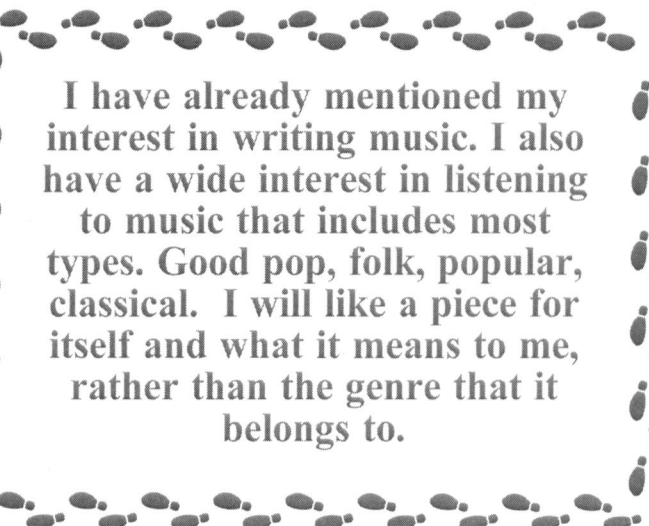

I have already mentioned my interest in writing music. I also have a wide interest in listening to music that includes most types. Good pop, folk, popular, classical. I will like a piece for itself and what it means to me, rather than the genre that it belongs to.

TO MUSIC

O great and mighty music!
O harmony divine!
You have the power to tear and rend
And soothe this soul of mine.

O happy, carefree music!
O syncopated tune!
You turn a winter's moodiness
Into a flash of June.

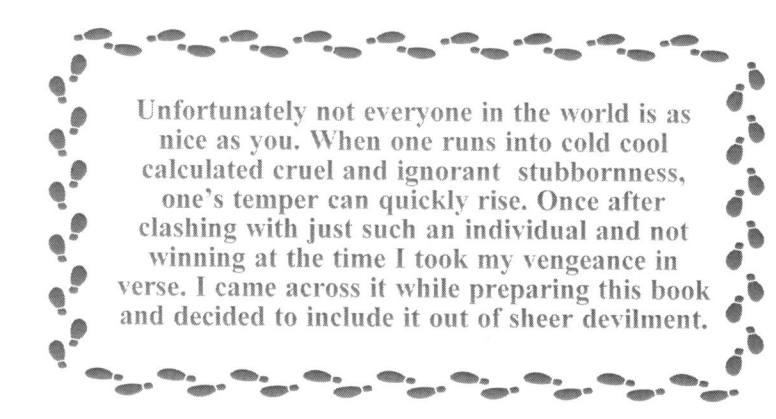

> Unfortunately not everyone in the world is as nice as you. When one runs into cold cool calculated cruel and ignorant stubbornness, one's temper can quickly rise. Once after clashing with just such an individual and not winning at the time I took my vengeance in verse. I came across it while preparing this book and decided to include it out of sheer devilment.

I wish I'd said that at the time.

You slight inconsequential man. When God
Gave wit, then you came second to a fool:
Gave sight, then you came second to a bat:
Gave humours, then you stood upon your head.
That in one life one man should suffer such,
Should so be plagued with all that in a man
Is viewed with scorn and unrestrained mirth
Could almost win my heart to pity you.
But arrogance and misbegotten pride
Like devils on a stubborn donkey sit
And curse all hope of understanding friends.
One can but hope that in his mercy God
May look the other way on judgement day.
Else Peter's sure to shut the heavenly doors
Before demeanours quite as mean as yours.

Through school years I was exposed to large quantities of poetry. I loved it. That was until I had a particular teacher whose teaching methods introduced an element of aversion therapy. We had to learn a poem and write it out perfectly the following day. For every mistake you would lose a mark out of 20. This would not only be wrong words but spelling mistakes, missing or wrong punctuation,un-crossed Ts and un-dotted Is. To be fair Dyslexia was not recognised in those days and all my mistakes were regarded as carelessness or idleness. 16 was the pass mark and you got 1 stroke of the cane for each mistake below that. I learnt to dread poetry. He was still teaching when I visited the school 20 years later. I walked up to him and said,"Despite the fact that you taught me to hate and fear poetry, I did get over it" I then turned and walked away.

Amongst my favourite poets were the war poets such as Rupert Brooke, Robert Graves,Rudyard Kipling, Siegfried Sassoon, etc. Almost in revenge against the damaging assaults of my English teacher I wrote "A Moment in War". Written in those far off days it is therefore one of my earliest poems.

A Moment in war

He stood
He gazed
He realized
A feeling inside him grew higher and higher
Till soon he could stand it no longer.
Like fire it o'rcame him.
And then in a moment he ran.

Before him saw all agrasp on the field
His brother
In his mind he could hear the soft callings and weepings
Their mother

With this thought he arrived
At his dear brother's side
Whom he quickly revived
For a time there they bide

Then with brother in arms he ran and he ran
With a mind now of calm.

A thundering rattle
Did finish their battle.

Hugh Timothy
(1955 aged 13)

Confession time! A few years ago I started writing a play that I have yet to finish. To avoid telling you the whole plot, I will just say that part of the play hung on the hero finding a poem scribbled in the back of an old book that he unearthed in a second-hand book shop. He believed from the title of the poem, the dilapidated state and age of the book that the poem had been written by a soldier in the trenches, during the first world war, waiting for the horrific charge in which so many died, known as The Push. The hero reads it to one of the other characters to get their opinion. Now the confession. I tried out the poem on the audience at the Folk Club that I mentioned previously. I told them the story of having found it in a book shop as though I had found it - not mentioning my play. Afterwards several people came to me and said "its obviously the real thing. It has to be". I was of course very pleased that others felt that it rang true. I kept up the pretence and said nothing. Just recently I read them the poem again and told the truth. I do sometimes wonder though, if after all perhaps some soldier that died in the trenches is in fact writing his poem through me. I certainly have always felt strange about it.

THE PUSH

And then the sun shone.
And we, who waited, saw it with our eyes,
Yet could not feel it with our souls.
Portentous Death was not made lighter by it,
Just `luminated brighter and still brighter.
We could have loved an all embracing fog
But sun, the joy of happy summer days
And crisp white winter mornings
Held not one ounce of joy for us
Who waited for the Push.
It could not warm us - dry our rotting feet.
The cold wet mud just thickened into sickly slime.
The sun brought out its colour.
That strange, strange tint that only blood could give it.
And we who saw it all with blanket eyes
Saw nothing more beyond but.......................

The inspiration for the next poem is me, before waking up again to life. Many people have told me that it is true for them too. Perhaps, if we are honest it is true for most of us at some time or other.

THE FENCE

"It's a long way down", he said
As he sat on the fence.

"What's more it's a long way down
on both sides", he worried.

"I can't even think how I got here,
So which side's home?"

"And what's on the other side,
Whichever that is?"

"If I do decide to get off,
Will I get down in one piece?"

"If I do get down in one piece,
Will it be the right side?"

"If I should get down on the wrong side,
How shall I know?"

"I may think I'm down on the right side
And then find I'm wrong".

"I may think I'm down on the wrong side
and be wrong `cos I'm right".

"I think I'll stay on the fence till something turns up.
It's a long way down".

The wind turned up and blew him off,
Much to his surprise.

It was then he found that the fence
Was just his imagination.

I mentioned earlier my love of Cornwall. I spent my first birthday on a beach called Daymer Bay situated in the mouth of the river Camel estuary facing both river and sea. Interestingly not 200 yards away on the cliff top above stood the home of the man who was later to become Poet Laureate, the late Sir John Betjeman. My love affair with Cornwall was to go on forever. Whilst nostalgia for childhood days is a part of it, it runs deeper than that. The hypnotic sea in all its seasons and moods, the constancy of the massive rocky landscape, was a sort of foundation in my own life and while there is of course continued erosion of the landscape, the over all feeling is one of immovability and permanence. The wonderful people of Cornwall are unique unto themselves, warm, friendly, stoic through all adversity and with a joy of singing matched only by their Celtic cousins the Welsh.

A little farther north from Daymer, the huge Hayle Bay, more commonly known as Polzeath, opens up, sweeping eastward in land, then round in a wide curve and out to Pentire, the further of the two headlands that mark entrance to the Camel estuary. A part of Polzeath, Tristram is a small side Bay facing Pentire. On Pentire, as on other Cornish headlands, can be found the remains of hill forts, built by early invaders as footholds before advancing inland.

Pentire from Tristram is the first of my Cornish poems.

PENTIRE FROM TRISTRAM

Powerful Pentire, Arm defiant,
Splits the timeless sea asunder.
Greets the raging ocean's onslaught
With a scorn, majestic, steadfast.

Stands unyielding, through the ages
Change so small can scarce be measured.
Only viewed across the aeons
Can be seen your alteration.

The parade of generations,
Down the path from man's arrival,
In your craggy granite splendour
Found new strength, cast in your image.

Where invaders on the cliff top
Made your battlements their fortress,
New invaders march along them
Armed with haversack and thermos.

Powerful hidden secret forces,
Wave and rock in interaction,
Fuel my mind, ignite my being,
Once again my soul recharging.

Sitting spellbound, I at Tristram,
Hear the voices of the ocean,
Thrown as echoes on the rock face
And as whispers on the shingle.

Habitat of whale and dolphin,
Seal and porpoise, clawed crustacean
World of mackerel and of weever
Tumbles madly round about me.

Jealously I sit and view it
Only wanting friends to share it.
Those who know it and remember
All the years we grew to love it.

Out across the bay to Pentire
Wave on wave the crashing water
Sweeping up the battling surfers
Swamps the laughter of the bathers.

Look now, along the waters' edge,
A mirror tide that ebbs and flows
A human ocean meets the sea
To try to match its endless pulse.

Hot lazy summer afternoons are a joy to capture in verse. The peace, the smells and noises of summer are a rich narcotic. But idleness can catch you out. It did once for someone I knew.

MIDSUMMER MADNESS

On a sunny summer Sunday
Lying on my back and gazing
At the clear cool blue of heaven
Balmy afternoon for lazing.

Almost listening to the cricket
Out across the field before me
Gentle breezes waft its noises,
Sound of distant ball on willow.

Silence - click then clap or shouting
Gentle wave of muffled laughter.
Far off their enthusiasm
Making my repose more peaceful.

Lying restful, slumber creeping
Lulls me gently, almost sleeping.
AWAKE WITH PAIN, my fingers fall
My stomach's caught a cricket ball!

I have no idea how the next poem originated. I know I wrote it and it must have been a long time ago. I am sure I must have written it with someone in mind but I can't think of anyone in my courting days that seems to match the thoughts. There is an uncertain recollection that it was in fact a dream that I put into verse, perhaps to try to sort out its meaning in my mind. I include it in part of ***Stepping into Verse*** as it is part of those very first steps.

VISION

And as I dreamed, I dreamed of her
And all about was black.
A golden vision stood alone,
With golden hair on gilded throne
And golden light shone from her eyes,
Yet all about was black.

And as I stood she beckoned me
And bade me come aside.
Yet I refused and stood alone
Before the jewelled and gilded throne
The vision with the golden eyes
And all about was black

Then through the black an angry mob
Swept in from every side.
They stripped her splendour and her throne,
Her wealth and fortune all were gone.
The golden eyes were full of fear,
But all about was light.

'Twas then my being swelled with joy.
I took her in my arms
And down the steps we walked alone
I took her from her world, now gone
And into one where living shone:
I led her into mine.

Eskimo Pete is no relation to the Eskimo lady whose name is the title of a certain notorious piece of verse. Eskimo Pete was written for performance at the folk club and was loosely based on a shaggy dog story I heard on the radio some 20 years earlier.

THE TALE OF ESKIMO PETE

I have a tale with moral old but true.
About a certain Eskimo called Pete,
Who had the little problem Eskimos
Can tend to get - He suffered from cold feet.

'Twas not so much when going walk-about,
For then his feet were always on the go.
'Twas when he went and took his kayak out
That cold crept slowly into every toe.

It caused him such distress that he resolved
To try out every remedy. In vain
He tried hot water bottles and thick socks;
In fact all thermal clothes he could obtain.

Then one day in the trading post he saw
A sight that sent his mind into a spin.
The answer lay before him on the floor;
A little stove that ran on paraffin.

He wasted not a second and installed
The little stove, that source of golden heat.
Never more when fishing to be cold.
Especially he'd have no more cold feet.

His pride and joy now burning near his feet,
He set off in his kayak seaward bound.............
DISASTER STRUCK, the stove set fire the boat.
The burning boat then sank and Pete was drowned.

THE MORAL

When by conflicting interests you're beset
And do not know what you should seek to do.
Remember then the moral of Pete's tale.
You cannot have your kayak and heat it too.

Back to Cornwall again for the next poem, in which I explored a bit more my feelings about its growing popularity and the changes that this has brought to this strong, rugged yet strangely fragile place. I, of course, see Cornwall through holidaymakers' eyes and am as guilty of the rape of Cornwall as all the others. But I was there first so it must be mine, mustn't it?

Polzeath Possessive

In 1952 the bay was ours.
That Great expanse of sand
Was all but empty. If you scanned
The rocks and cliffs around the bay
Perhaps a party here a couple there
A child at play.

Heaven was here. We knew it too.
The sea we shared with God. The sun, the spray
That crashed upon the rocks then dried away.
Each north Atlantic day of endless waves,
Withstood or swept away,
With topsy-turvy gurgling laughter.

And as the lazy day wore on there might be seen
Some walker on a cliff top stroll
Roaming the headland's soft and spongy green

We loved it so
And told our friends and so did they,
And now the bay is full to bursting.
And tens of thousand feet
Are trekking every head.
So now the cliff top green
Is worn away in such a way
As never spray or rain could do.

Do you believe in reincarnation - that the soul can be reborn again in a new body.

About 20 years ago I got to know a lovely young lady who seriously considered that she might have been Joan of Arc in a previous life. She used to experience vivid flashbacks to those days. Often in her childhood she had awoken screaming from a dream of burning at the stake. If she had told her story as one of a string of fanciful tales I would have given it no credence but it was the "What-do you-think-'cos-I-don't-know" way she had of telling me about it that fascinated me enough to explore her story in a little depth. It was thinking about all this and the real Joan, that lead to the next poem.

LA PUCELLE

The Maid who wandered barefoot through the woods
And took the song of nature to her heart.
The wild thing loved alike by all wild things,
Who worshipped in her turn wild nature's art.

The maid who gave herself to tend the sick,
Whose gentle ministrations served as balm
For every wounded soldier in her care,
The living and the dying in her arm.

The maid who heard the voice and made a king,
Nor thought it strange, nor wondered at the deed.
A peasant girl who steeled the soldiers' hearts
In armour clad she lead them on a steed.

The maid who found her king a broken reed.
Betrayed, declared a heretic and fake.
In body gaoled and in the spirit too.
Then in the market square burned at the stake.

What essence in these ashes can be found?
Here is the daughter of the love of man.
For here lies innocence and faith sweet mixed.
For to the slaughter came another Lamb.

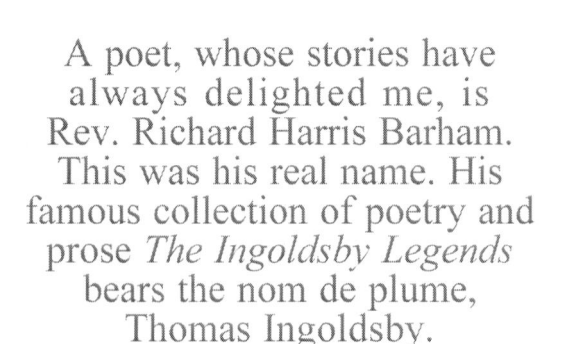

A poet, whose stories have always delighted me, is Rev. Richard Harris Barham. This was his real name. His famous collection of poetry and prose *The Ingoldsby Legends* bears the nom de plume, Thomas Ingoldsby.

My grandfather introduced me, at an early age, to such delicious stories in verse as *The Knight and the Lady, The Jackdaw of Rheims, and Look at the Clock*, which held me spellbound for hours on end.

The Ingoldsby influence on the next poem cannot be denied. It was deliberate.

A LEGEND OF ST CECILIA

Barnstaple Brown had that look in his eye
   Of a man who on pleasure was bent.
   And the spring of his step was exceedingly spry
Whilst his manner was blithe and content.
   But this aura of glee,   To a marked degree
Suggested a man who was off on a spree.
   And hardly surprising,   This look compromising
His plans were just what they appeared they might be.

   At this juncture I fear,   I should make it quite clear
That his earnest pursuit after beer and good cheer
Was not the exception so much as the rule
Which he shared with a keen bacchanalian school.
For the target and aim of the group was quite plain: it
Was enter a pub and then post haste to drain it.

There were some who would go to some pains to express
How the thought it a gross and disgusting excess:
   But Barnstaple's crew   Held a quite different view,
And in no way regarded their habit "taboo".
   On the contrary, they,   When questioned would say
They considered their practice a very fine way
Of making the temperance movement effective:
For Barnstaple Brown and his drinking collective,
In drinking pubs dry made the self same objective.
At the risk of lab'ring the point, I'll make plain,
That pubs with no liquor no customers stay in.

    These great boozers and true, To give them their due,
Were not really disturbed by the temperance view.
    Their purpose was fixed, (If their manners were mixed):
Their aim was not only solely consumption of liquor:
Their plan was much broader, considerably bigger.
I hope my sad rhyming won't cause us to bicker....
But really, the problems a poet can meet with
Are a trial you'll admit, it is hard to compete with).

But I fancy I wander so back to my tale:
Apart from the practice of drinking strong ale,
Each man considered himself to be really a
Perfect disciple of blessed St Cecilia.
For myself I can't say I'm averse to a song;
Be it pretty and short or balladic and long.
But I must admit their songs lacked much in propriety,
And are rarely indulged in female society.
 For I'm sure that their songs, when the sweet air they clave,
Were enough to make any saint turn in their grave.

Each song on a melody famous depends.
But there, at that point, the resemblance ends.
    The Lyrics are barmy;   Lacking totally in charm. I
Suspect that they mostly came out of the army,
Or air force, or Navy, Or Rugby club tub;
And after the shower room down at the pub.
For where ever violence or mayhem has ruled
You will always find men who are very well schooled
In the songs Barnie Brown and his friends gaily sang,
With their liberal use of those old words that sprang
From the Angles and Saxons' most primitive slang.

That particular night,   he mood being right,
They'd become very quickly what you'd define tight.
   So that by twelve o'clock,   It was not a great shock -
(All public-house doors being firmly on lock)
To find that our party are taking the air,
And wandering home very much worse for wear.
   Yet despite their excess,   They are still none the less
Singing heartily: truly for me to express
The extent of their heartiness I'll not asperse,
Save to say that it made the whole neighbourhood curse.
From windows came comments both pithy and terse.
If roof there had been they'd have raised it or worse.
So they set about raising the whole universe.

The route they took home I shall not dissert on:
The paths, that a drunk takes are ne'er at best certain.
My reference is drawn from G. K. Chesterton,
Who reckoned as I do that each rambling road
Of our great British countryside certainly owed
A great deal to the drunk and the path that he strode;
From our mead-bewitched forefathers covered in woad
To the motorist whom the police car has slowed
To a stop and the bag he would love to explode.
   Suffice it to say,   That their wandering way
Led them into the churchyard; a place, one would say,
Was most inappropriate for their roundelay.

   This particular song -   They were going it strong -
Was reaching its climax. Now don't get me wrong.
The climax to their ears was tres magnifique
To your or to my ears in harmony weak.

Some people sing sharpish and others sing flat.
Put them together - preserve me from that! -
And the final effect is a ghastly cacophony,
Which is enough to put anyone off. Any
Small trace of music is lost in the row.
Should the singers be drunk, then its much worse - and how!

The song is now over, its last note grown faint,
When who should appear in their midst but the Saint,
    Eyes blazing with ire,   Like two coals of fire.
This beautiful maiden in Roman attire,
Saint Cecilia stood there before them in wrath:
In demeanour and attitude barring their path.
    That look in her eyes,   All movement defies.
So having o'rcome their initial surprise
    They became, as you'll hear - 'Twas abundantly clear -
Paralytic with fear as they had been with beer.

With her hand raised on high, a known predilection
Of saints when pronouncing a nice benediction,
Or to fortify curses with greater conviction,
She spoke. Now when angry were all apt to make
In our haste some slightly embarrassing mistake.
So did our saint and though it sounds absurd,
Barnie and friends couldn't make out a word.
For in haste she had chosen to furnish her chat in
Her local familiar third century Latin.

The effect that this had on the group, you'll surmise,
Were expressions of horror, mixed well with surprise.
Till finally mystery showed in their eyes.
'Twas this look of incredulous wonder that gave
St. Cecilia the hint that if souls she would save,
'Twould be wise that she phrase her address in the tongue
And the style of the folk she was preaching among.

So beginning again   in the Anglican strain
She made clear to the group the great anger and pain
That their singing inflicted on sanctified ears
Her message did nought towards calming their fears,
But made it quite plain, if they stuck to their beers,
On Great Judgement Day to hell they'd be banished;
Then quick as she came Saint Cecilia vanished.

I need hardly describe the mood in her wake
Save that Barnstaple's Cronies did quiver and shake;
And made for their homes, with shrieks and with wails
As quick as if Old Nick was close on their tails.
That night, as each man to bed went, he swore
Never ales wines or spirits he'd drink any more.
And their stern resolution `twould be fair to say
Lasted precisely two weeks and a day.
The call of the bottle too strong to resist.
They returned to the drinking and promptly got pissed.

   Two weeks on the waggon   Without dram or flagon
Makes a great thirst and resolve tends to flag. On
That night they succeeded in downing with zest
All they could have consumed in their fortnight long rest.
So the mood they were in, when at last shown the door,
Was far more unruly than ever before.
When the church yard was reached by the booze-ridden party,
Their singing, still bawdy, was even more hearty.
Whether bravado encouraged their song:
Liquor brings courage when drunk good and strong,
And certainly dulls any clear recollection.
It makes folk rebellious and breeds insurrection.
For riot is the only word apt to describe
The behaviour of Banstable Brown and his tribe.

Now the patience of saints is well known to us all.
-But fear not good reader, I shall not recall
The hundreds of saints, and listing each case in full
The trials that they met with that came by the basinful;
I'll only remind you that saints, unlike us,
Are not quickly upset by a bit of a fuss.
So you'll see that the shocking and unholy row
That disturbed Saint Cecilia so deeply, (and how
She determined to punish such wickedness dearly)
Was greatly beyond what people would clearly
Call normal. So gathering her robes round her tight
She popped up in the church yard and gave them a fright.

Before she'd been angry as all would avow,
But her fury was many times magnified now:
And I don't think it's being unfair to the soul
To suggest a slight loss of her great self control.
That familiar gesture, that hand in the air,
Was accompanied now by a curse, which I swear
Has never been matched for professional flair,
Nor for content most damning and full of despair.
'Twas not verbal inflation
This saints condemnation.
Full of edification
Her expostulation
Gave stern reprobation
And fierce castigation
No justification
For intoxication
Their gross violation
Of her intimation
At this same location
Was just provocation
For her imprecation
They had earned and would get IN<u>ST</u>ANT termination.

In short Saint Cecilia made it quite clear
'Twas the end not just of their drinking career,
But their mortal existence and all they held dear.
With just one exception - a very strange thing -
They were doomed from that time to eternally sing
Not in heaven or hell but the scene of their crime.
To endlessly act out the whole pantomime.

   From that day to this,   Not a night do they miss;
Excepting the Sabbath when 'twould be remiss
They are chanting away still some sharp and some flat, in
Not English at all but Cecilia's Latin.

   There's a good chance 'tis said,   As you go home to bed,
That you'll see them yourself, if you've not learnt from my
Advice in these matters, and you should pass by
Having spent the whole evening drinking pubs dry.

I finish with a poem I wrote only a few weeks before I began preparing this collection. I was walking down a lane and this blackbird started singing at me. I spoke to him and he sang again. After he had flown away, the poem arrived in my head almost complete. The title seemed appropriate to end with if you know what I mean?

Bye-Bye Blackbird

I met a Blackbird in the lane
And stopped to have a chat.
He talked a lot of blackbirdese
And trilled of this and that.

I asked him how he found the world?
His song was pure and gay.
He then politely bobbed his head
And singing flew away.

But now they've built the motorway
With factories all around.
I saw a blackbird in the lane,
Dead upon the ground.